Seven
CONTINENTS
of the World

NORTH AMERICA

By Tracy Vonder Brink

A Crabtree Crown Book

School-to-Home Support for Caregivers and Teachers

This appealing book is designed to teach students about core subject areas. Students will build upon what they already know about the subject, and engage in topics that they want to learn more about. Here are a few guiding questions to help readers build their comprehensions skills. Possible answers appear here in red.

Before Reading:
What do I know about North America?
- *I know North America is a continent.*
- *I know bears live in North America.*

What do I want to learn about this topic?
- *I want to know how many countries are in North America.*
- *I want to learn about animals that live in North America.*

During Reading:
I'm curious to know...
- *I'm curious to know what kind of foods North Americans eat.*
- *I'm curious to know what sports North Americans enjoy.*

How is this like something I already know?
- *I know what foods people who live near me eat.*
- *I know what sports I like to play.*

After Reading:
What was the author trying to teach me?
- *The author was trying to teach me what kind of landforms North America has.*
- *The author was trying to teach me about North American countries.*

How did the photographs and captions help me understand more?
- *The photographs helped me picture North America.*
- *The captions gave me extra information.*

TABLE OF CONTENTS

CHAPTER 1
Get to Know North America 4

CHAPTER 2
Landforms and Climate 8

CHAPTER 3
Natural Resources 14

CHAPTER 4
Plants and Animals 16

CHAPTER 5
Countries and Cities 22

CHAPTER 6
Culture and People 26

GLOSSARY 30

INDEX 31

COMPREHENSION QUESTIONS 31

ABOUT THE AUTHOR 32

CHAPTER 1
GET TO KNOW NORTH AMERICA

What continent has the largest area of freshwater in the world? Where do bald eagles fly and pronghorns run? Where do more than 500 million people live?

North America!

North America is north of the **equator**. The continent extends from the Arctic Circle in the north almost to the equator in the south. North America is wide at the top and narrows as it nears South America.

The world has seven continents. North America is the third largest.

OCEANS AND ISLANDS

The Arctic Ocean **borders** the continent's north. The Caribbean Sea lies to its south. The Atlantic Ocean splashes against its eastern side. The Pacific Ocean is to its west. Island chains, such as the Caribbean Islands and the Hawaiian Islands, are also part of North America.

Oahu is the third largest Hawaiian island.

Seven countries make up Central America. They are Belize, Guatemala, El Salvador, Honduras, Nicaragua, Costa Rica, and Panama.

CENTRAL AMERICA

The Isthmus of Panama is a narrow strip of land between the Pacific Ocean and the Caribbean Sea. It connects North and South America. This region is often called Central America, but it is still part of North America.

CHAPTER 2
LANDFORMS AND CLIMATE

North America has rugged mountains and massive grasslands. The continent also has a large, rocky **plateau**. Lakes and rivers supply the land with water.

North America has tropical rain forests, but it also has cooler temperate rain forests. Temperate rain forests are not near the equator. Their water comes from clouds, fog, and rain.

The Rockies are the longest North American mountain range. They are also one of the longest mountain ranges in the world.

MOUNTAINS

The Rocky Mountains begin in the northern part of western Canada and end in New Mexico. The Appalachian Mountains start in eastern Canada and extend into the southern United States. The Sierra Madre mountain range crosses from Mexico into Central America.

PLAINS

Grasslands cover parts of ten U.S. states and three Canadian **provinces**. These grasslands are known as the Great **Plains**. The Great Plains are mostly flat, but some areas have hills and low mountains.

Bison are the largest animals in the Great Plains.

Canada and the United States share Niagara Falls. Three waterfalls make up Niagara Falls. They are American Falls, Bridal Veil Falls, and Horseshoe Falls.

WATERS

North America has large bodies of water. The Missouri River flows through the Great Plains in the United States. The Saskatchewan is the main river in the Canadian part of the plains. The Great Lakes are in eastern and central North America. They are the world's largest area of freshwater.

A ROCKY PLATEAU

The Canadian Shield covers almost half of Canada. This area of rock is more than 540 million years old. The Canadian Shield contains mountain ranges, lakes, and rivers. It also has one of the world's largest forests.

The Canadian Yukon sees the coldest temperatures in North America. The Yukon has been as cold as -84°F (-63°C). Death Valley, a desert in the U.S., is the hottest. It was once 134°F (56.7°C).

CLIMATE

North America stretches from far in the north to deep in the south, so it contains different climates. Alaska and parts of northern Canada are cold Arctic regions. The Great Plains have warm summers and cold winters. Central America stays warm and tropical all year.

CHAPTER 3
NATURAL RESOURCES

Minerals such as copper, silver, lead, and iron ore are found in North America. The United States, Canada, and Mexico all contain coal. These countries also have oil. Coal and oil are important sources of energy and fuel.

Wheat is used to make bread, pasta, crackers, and much more.

The continent sells its crops around the world. The United States grows fresh fruits and vegetables such as apples, grapes, and lettuce. The United States and Canada produce wheat, corn, and soybeans. Central America grows coffee beans, sugar, and bananas.

CHAPTER 4
PLANTS AND ANIMALS

Birds, bears, and deer may eat wild cranberries.

Spruce and fir trees are evergreen trees that keep their leaves all year.

PLANTS

North American plants are different from region to region. No trees grow in the Arctic regions of Alaska and Canada. Tall grasses fill the Great Plains. Orchids bloom in Central American rain forests.

Spruce and fir trees grow tall in Canada's forests. Wild cranberry shrubs make bright-red berries. The United States once cut down its forests for wood and cleared land for homes and farms. Now the country has national forests that are protected areas.

ANIMALS OF THE FOREST

Black and brown bears roam through North American forests. Grizzly bears are a type of brown bear found in coastal forests. Moose make their homes in forests near lakes, ponds, or streams. Bald eagles catch fish in big lakes near forests.

The United States has protected spaces. But some animals, such as the grizzly bear, are still in danger of dying out.

Squirrel monkeys are small. Adults are between 9 to 14 inches (23-36 cm) tall.

Sloths sleep in the tropical trees of the Central American rain forests. Squirrel monkeys squeak, and scarlet macaws flap their colorful wings. Jaguars hunt in these rain forests. They are the largest cat in Central America.

ANIMALS OF THE NORTH

Polar bears live in the Arctic regions of Alaska and Canada. They hunt different **species** of seals there. Arctic ground squirrels are the largest North American ground squirrel. They hibernate for about eight months a year. Snowy owls feed on ground squirrels and other small animals.

North American tropical islands are the opposite of the cold Arctic. Coral reefs grow off the coasts of the Hawaiian and Caribbean islands. Sea turtles, dolphins, and many kinds of fish swim there.

ANIMALS OF THE GREAT PLAINS

Pronghorns are the fastest North American land animals. They sprint across the plains. Black-tailed prairie dogs burrow in the soil. Millions of bison, also called buffalo, once roamed the Great Plains. They were nearly wiped out when settlers moved west. Today, some herds are protected to try and grow their numbers.

CHAPTER 5
COUNTRIES AND CITIES

The island nation of Saint Kitts and Nevis is the smallest North American country. Around 53,000 people live there. It also has the least amount of land of any North American country.

COUNTRIES

North America is made up of 23 countries. Canada has the most land of any North American country. The United States has the most people. More than 300 million people live in the United States. Mexico is the second most **populous** country. It has more than 130 million people.

North America has a big gap between its richest and poorest nations. Some, such as the United States and Canada, produce many goods and have many jobs. Other countries, such as Haiti and Nicaragua, suffer from widespread **poverty**.

CITIES

In North America, most people live in cities. Only around 20% make their homes in the countryside. Mexico City has the most people of any city in North America. More than 20 million people live there. New York City has almost as many.

Guanajuato, Mexico, is known for its silver mines.

Big cities offer better jobs, more schools, and more opportunities. But cities are also often overcrowded. Some who live there are very poor, even in the richest countries. Cars and factories may dirty the air.

CHAPTER 6
CULTURE AND PEOPLE

Indigenous peoples were the first to live in North America. Their civilizations date back thousands of years. Then explorers and settlers from Europe came and took the Indigenous peoples' lands for their own. Today, Indigenous peoples still fight for their rights.

> Millions of enslaved Africans were brought to North America and forced to work. Later, they gained their freedom. Today many people in North America have African heritage.

North America has a wide mix of cultures. Indigenous peoples have their own traditions. European settlers brought the traditions of their home countries with them. Immigrants from other countries continue to move to the continent. Hundreds of languages are spoken in North America, although English and Spanish are the most common.

FOOD

Many North American foods came from other continents, but some are unique. Canadians enjoy poutine, gravy and cheese curds tossed with fries. Chocolate chip cookies were invented in the United States. Tortillas and tamales come from the Indigenous cultures of Mexico and Central America.

Poutine is so popular in Canada that it's on the menu at McDonald's.

SPORTS

North Americans love sports. In the United States, baseball, basketball, and football are popular. Canadians love ice hockey. Soccer is played around the continent but is most popular in Mexico and Central America.

GLOSSARY

border (BOR-dr): The place where one area ends and another starts

equator (EE-kway-tr): An imaginary line around the middle of Earth that is the same distance from the North Pole to the South Pole

Indigenous (in-DIH-juh-nuhs): The first people who lived in any region and not later immigrants

mineral (MIH-nuh-rl): A solid substance that is formed naturally under the ground

plains (PLAYNZ): A large stretch of mostly flat land

plateau (pla-TOW): A broad area of high, flat land

populous (PAW-pyuh-luhs): Having a large population

poverty (PAH-vr-tee): The state of being poor, or lacking money

province (PRAH-vince): A large part of a country with its own government

species (SPEE-sheez or SPEE-sees): A group of animals or plants that are alike in certain ways

INDEX

Canada 9, 11-15, 17, 20, 23, 28, 29

Canadian Shield 12

Caribbean 6-7, 20

Central America 7, 9, 13-15, 17, 19, 28-29

Great Plains 10-11, 13, 17, 21

Indigenous 26-28

Mexico 9, 14, 23-24, 28-29

Niagara Falls 11

Rocky Mountains 9

United States 9-11, 14-15, 17-18, 23, 28-29

COMPREHENSION QUESTIONS

1. How many people live in North America?
    a. More than 500 million
    b. More than 1 billion
    c. About 100 million

2. Which animal lives in the North American forests?
    a. Pronghorn
    b. Polar bear
    c. Brown bear

3. What country has the most people in North America?
    a. Mexico
    b. The United States
    c. Canada

4. True or False: All of North America lies below the equator.

5. True of False: Central America is a separate continent from North America.

Answers: 1. A, 2. C, 3. B, 4. False, 5. False

ABOUT THE AUTHOR

Tracy Vonder Brink loves true stories and facts. She has written more than 20 books for kids and is a contributing editor for three children's science magazines. Tracy lives in Cincinnati, Ohio, with her husband, two daughters, and two rescue dogs.

Written by: Tracy Vonder Brink
Cover design by: Kathy Walsh
Interior design by: Kathy Walsh
Series Development: James Earley
Proofreader: Crystal Sikkens
Educational Consultant: Marie Lemke M.Ed.
Print coordinator: Katherine Berti

Photographs: Shutterstock; Cover: ©Triff, ©Khurasan, ©nypl, @Dima_designer, ©David Rasmus; Title Pg: ©Triff, ©Dima_designer; Pg 3-31: ©Triff; Pg 4-31: ©Margarita Steshnikova; Pg 4: ©i viewfinder; Pg 6: ©Damien VERRIER; Pg 7: ©Lucy.Brown; Pg 8: ©YegoroV; Pg 9: ©kavram; Pg 10: nyker; Pg 11: ©lastdjedai; Pg 12: ©Marc Filion; Pg 13: ©davidrh; Pg 14: ©Kristi Blokhin; Pg 15: ©Aleksandr Rybalko; Pg 16: ©Greens and Blues; Pg 17: ©Gestalt Imagery; Pg 18: ©Dennis W Donohue; Pg 19: ©George Arenas, ©l i g h t p o e t; Pg 20: ©David Carbo; Pg 21: ©Kyle Spradley Photography, ©l i g h t p o e t; Pg 22: ©NAPA; Pg 23: ©Daniel-Alvarez; Pg 24: ©alberto cervantes; Pg 25: ©Frontpage; Pg 26: ©Pierre Jean Durieu; Pg 27: © Rawpixel.com; Pg 28: ©FILMME; Pg 29: ©mTaira

Library and Archives Canada Cataloguing in Publication
Available at the Library and Archives Canada

Library of Congress Cataloging-in-Publication Data
Available at the Library of Congress

Crabtree Publishing Company
www.crabtreebooks.com   1-800-387-7650

Copyright © 2023 **CRABTREE PUBLISHING COMPANY**

All rights reserved. No part of this publication may be reproduced, stored in a retrieval system or be transmitted in any form or by any means, electronic, mechanical, photocopying, recording, or otherwise, without the prior written permission of Crabtree Publishing Company. In Canada: We acknowledge the financial support of the Government of Canada through the Canada Book Fund for our publishing activities.

Published in the United States
Crabtree Publishing
347 Fifth Avenue
Suite 1402-145
New York, NY, 10016

Published in Canada
Crabtree Publishing
616 Welland Ave.
St. Catharines, ON
L2M 5V6

Printed in the U.S.A./072022/CG20220201